To:

_____

From:

_____

Date:

_____

Joyful Blessings for Someone Special

© 2013 Christian Art Gifts, RSA
          Christian Art Gifts Inc., IL, USA

Designed by Christian Art Gifts

Images used under license from Shutterstock.com

Scripture quotations are taken from the *Holy Bible*, New International Version®
NIV®. Copyright © 1973, 1978, 1984, 2011 by International Bible Society. Used by
permission of Zondervan Publishing House. All rights reserved.

Scripture quotations are taken from the *Holy Bible*, New Living Translation®, second
edition. Copyright © 1996, 2004 by Tyndale House Publishers, Inc., Carol Stream,
Illinois 60188. All rights reserved.

Printed in China

ISBN 978-1-4321-0461-0

13   14   15   16   17   18   19   20   12   22   ²   12   11   10   9   8   7   6   5   4   3

Joyful Blessings
for *Someone*
Special

christian
art gifts®

Now these three remain: faith, hope and love. But the greatest of these is love.

– 1 Cor. 13:13 –

To *love* and
be loved is to
feel the sun from
both sides.

– David Viscott –

Though our feelings come and go God's love for us does not. – C. S. Lewis –

Perfect love
drives out
fear.

– 1 John 4:18 –

Love feels
no burden,
thinks nothing
of trouble,
attempts what
is above its
strength, pleads
no excuse of
impossibility.

– Thomas à Kempis –

A friend is a *treasure,*
More precious than gold,
for love shared is *priceless*
and never grows old.

– Anonymous –

God loves
each of us
as if there
were only
one of us.

– St. Augustine –

The Lord will take
great *delight* in you;
in His love He will *rejoice*
over you with singing.

– Zeph. 3:17 –

When the world says,
"Give up," Hope whispers,
"Try it one more time."

- Anonymous -

Let us *love one another,*
for *love comes from God.*
Everyone who loves
has been born of God
and knows God.

– 1 John 4:7 –

Keep the joy of loving
God in your heart and
share this joy with all
you meet, especially
your family.

– Mother Teresa –

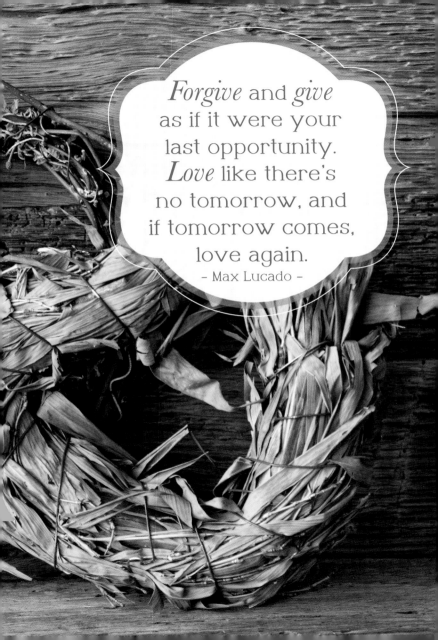

Forgive and *give*
as if it were your
last opportunity.
Love like there's
no tomorrow, and
if tomorrow comes,
love again.

– Max Lucado –

Spread love wherever you go ... Let no one ever come to you without leaving better and happier. Be the living expression of God's kindness.

– Mother Teresa –

If we love one another, God lives in us and *His love is made complete* in us.

– 1 John 4:12 –

Love never gives up, never loses faith,
is always hopeful, and endures
through every circumstance.
Love will last forever!
1 Cor. 13:7–8

Do everything in love. 1 Cor. 16:14

Do everything in love. 1 Cor. 16:14

Do everything in love. 1 Cor. 16:14

Give thanks to the LORD,
for He is good!
His faithful love endures forever.

"I have *loved* you,
with an *everlasting love.*
With *unfailing love* I have
drawn you to Myself."

– Jer. 31:3 –

What *great love*
the Father has
lavished on us,
that we should be
called *children of God!*
And that is
what we are!

– 1 John 3:1 –

I *thank* my God every
time I *remember* you.

– Phil. 1:3 –

No one has
ever seen God;
but if we love
one another,
God lives in us
and His love
is made
complete in us.

– 1 John 4:12 –

Nothing will separate us from the love of God ...

I am convinced that
neither death nor life,
neither angels nor demons,
neither the present nor
the future, nor any
powers, neither height
nor depth, nor anything
else in all creation, will be
able to separate us from
the love of God that is in
Christ Jesus our Lord.

– Rom 8:35, 38–39 –

To love is to find pleasure in the happiness of the person loved.

– Baron von Leibnitz –

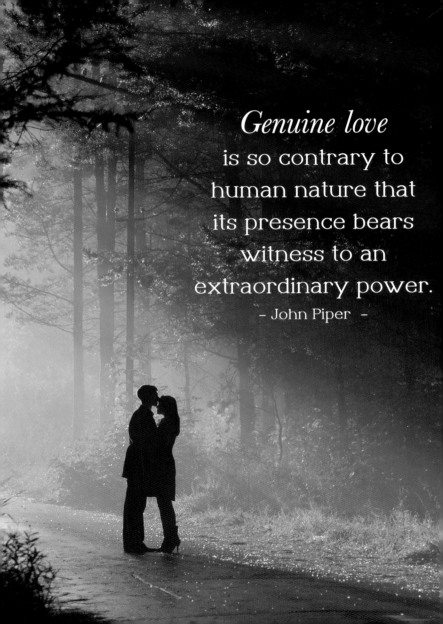

Genuine love is so contrary to human nature that its presence bears witness to an extraordinary power.

– John Piper –

And over all these virtues put on love, which binds them all together in perfect unity. – Col. 3:14 –

You have a
special place
in my heart.

– Phil. 1:7 –

"For God so *loved* the world that He gave His *one and only Son,* that whoever believes in Him shall not perish but have *eternal life."*

– John 3:16 –

38

"*Greater love* has
no one than this:
to lay down one's life
for one's friends."
– John 15:13 –

The *strength of love* is
shown in great things;
the *tenderness of love*
in little things.
– Robert C. Chapman –

Love does not consist in *gazing* at *each other,* but in *looking outward* together in the *same direction.*

– Antoine de Saint-Exupéry –

Two are better than one,
because they have a
good return for their labor:
If either of them falls down,
one can *help* the other up.
A cord of three strands
is not quickly broken.

– Eccles. 4:9–10, 12 –

There is no *difficulty* that
enough love will not *conquer;*
no *disease* that
enough love will not *heal;*
no *door* that
enough love will not *open;*
no *gulf* that
enough love will not *bridge;*
no *wall* that
enough love will not *throw down;*
no *sin* that
enough love will not *redeem.*

– Emmet Fox –

Pure love
is a
willingness
to give
without a
thought of
receiving
anything
in return.

– Peace Pilgrim –

Many waters cannot quench love; rivers cannot sweep it away. — Song of Songs 8:7 —

The love we give
away is the only
love we keep.

– Elbert Hubbard –